What IS FEMINISM?

Why do WE need it?

other & BIG QUESTIONS

Published in paperback in 2017 by Wayland

ISBN: 978 0 7502 9838 4
10 9 8 7 6 5 4 3 2 1

Printed in China

Wayland
An imprint of
Hachette Children's Group
Part of Hodder & Stoughton
Carmelite House
50 Victoria Embankment
London EC4Y 0DZ

An Hachette UK Company
www.hachette.co.uk
www.hachettechildrens.co.uk

Editor: Elizabeth Brent
Designer: Lisa Peacock
Cover design: Dynamo Ltd

The website addresses (URLs) included in this book were valid at the time of going to press. However, it is possible that contents or addresses may have changed since the publication of this book. No responsibility for any such changes can be accepted by either the author or the Publisher.

Picture acknowledgements: p4 Andrea Raffin/Shutterstock.com; p5 Suki Dhanda/ The Observer (bottom right); p7 DFree/Shutterstock.com; p9 DFree/Shutterstock.com; p12 Ann Ronan Pictures/Print Collector/Getty Images; p13 Susan Wood/Getty Images; p15 DFree/Shutterstock.com (top), Featureflash/Shutterstock.com (bottom); p19 Joseph Sohm/Shutterstock.com; p23 Jun Sato/WireImage; p26 Archive Holdings INC/Getty Images; p27 Tinseltown/Shutterstock.com; p28 Pete Niesen/Shutterstock. com; p29 Featureflash/Shutterstock.com (top), Andrew Toth/FilmMagic (bottom); p33 JStone/Shutterstock.com; p36 Sam Aronov/Shutterstock.com (bottom); p37 Everett Collection/Shutterstock.com; p38 Suki Dhanda/The Observer; p41 Everett Collection/ Shutterstock.com

Contents

Have you ever asked yourself, 'Are boys and girls really that different?', 'Why are most world leaders men?' or 'Why don't men wear skirts?' The aim of this book is to get you to think about questions like these, and to see how they affect your life and the lives of people all over the world.

INTRODUCING
Feminism

WHY DO WE NEED THIS BOOK?

You may have heard the word 'feminism' before, and wondered what it means. Or perhaps you know a little about it and would like to know more. People have very different ideas about what feminism is and what feminists – people who support equality and the rights of women – are like. This book is going to explain what feminism means and why it exists.

Many people don't think of themselves as feminists, but they still believe that both men and women should have equal rights and opportunities, and want girls to have the same choices and chances as boys. These people might not call themselves feminists, but they believe in feminist ideas. The aim of this book is to help you to understand what feminist ideas are and what feminism stands for.

> *When at 15, my girlfriends started dropping out of their beloved sports teams, because they didn't want to appear muscly, when at 18, my male friends were unable to express their feelings, I decided that I was a feminist.*

Emma Watson,
Actor and UN Women Goodwill Ambassador

HOW THE *book works*

In this book, we'll look at the history of women's equality, and at some of the amazing stories of men and women who brought about change.

We'll look into the areas of life where women have been, and in many cases still are, treated differently to men. We'll see what feminism has done to change attitudes and laws, and also tackle some big questions, for example, 'Can men be feminists too?' and 'Do we still need feminism today?'

Feminists in the public eye such as Gemma Cairney, Julie Bentley, Adora Svitak, Ben Bailey Smith (AKA Doc Brown), Lauren Laverne and Dawn O'Porter have all written about what feminism means to them and how it has affected their lives. Their stories are spread throughout the book, too. Along the way, you will also find quotes from other people who have said inspiring things about feminism, and questions to get you thinking as you read.

What is a FEMINIST?

A feminist is someone who believes that men and women should be treated equally. Feminists believe that, historically, women have had less power and fewer choices than men, that this is wrong and should be changed. There are different kinds of feminists, who have slightly different ideas about how these problems could be solved, but all feminists share the same basic belief that men and women shouldn't be treated differently just because they're male or female.

WORDS FEMINISTS USE

Patriarchy is a family, group or government that is controlled by a man or a group of men. In a patriarchy, men have more power than women and more control over making rules and laws. For example, in a patriarchal family, men make most of the decisions.

Gender discrimination is when people are treated differently because they are male or female. Gender is the behaviour associated with being a man or a woman. Gender discrimination is usually used to mean the unfair treatment of women.

Sexism is another word for gender discrimination. Sexist attitudes, behaviours and conditions try to dictate what women can and can't do, based on their gender.

A misogynist is a person who dislikes or is strongly prejudiced against women. A misogynist treats women as inferior to men, and is negative towards them.

There is a lot of misunderstanding surrounding what feminism is and what feminists believe. Here are some facts about what feminism does and does not mean to the majority of feminists:

- Feminists believe that women are due the same pay and the same chance to succeed in their chosen career as men
- Feminists believe that women should play an equal role in the governments that make the laws in their countries
- Feminists believe that stereotypes, such as the belief that all men are strong and brave while all women are gentle and weak, are wrong and harmful to both men and women
- Feminism is not about disliking or hating men. Feminists have partners, husbands, sons, friends and relatives who are men and who they like or love very much
- Feminists don't want to take power away from men or to control men. Feminism is about sharing power equally.

" *We all fight over what the label 'feminism' means but for me it's about empowerment. It's not about being more powerful than men – it's about having equal rights with protection, support, justice. It's about very basic things. It's not a badge like a fashion item.* **"**

Annie Lennox,
Singer-songwriter

MY *feminism*
BEA APPLEBY

Bea Appleby is a writer and editor who for many years worked on magazines for girls. She is now editor of The Female Lead, which is a campaign dedicated to celebrating women's achievements.

I have cared about feminism ever since I was a little girl. My mum is a great feminist role model – she was strong, successful and taught me that women should earn their own money and never depend on a man for security and freedom. My dad believed the same, and he and my mum were equal at home.

But when I watched TV and films I saw a different world. Women didn't seem equal to men at all! They were often playing weak, delicate characters, and they were always very pretty. I wondered, is being beautiful the most important thing women can be? If so, that's really very boring.

I also wondered – women make up 50 per cent of the world, why don't they do 50 per cent of the jobs? Why do women wear high heels that they can't run for a bus in? Why don't men? Why do girls play with dolls and boys play with cars? Why do women wear make-up, but men can't?

It didn't seem fair, and still doesn't seem fair, that women were less powerful in the world. Trying to change that is what feminism means to me – having the power to decide what happens to the world we live in, to our bodies, how we behave and whether we are safe. Nowhere in the world are men and women truly equal.

WHAT *drives me now*

Feminism became part of my work when I was editor of a pre-teen magazine called *Girl Talk*. It seemed like everything in that magazine was pink, because it was for girls, and all the features were about fashion, hairstyles and pop stars. I worried that girls reading it would think that they had to be cute, pretty and nothing else.

So I started a campaign to make that magazine feminist – to include stories about sportswomen and scientists, to show all the amazing careers girls can have, from computer-game designers to racing drivers. I wanted the magazine to tell girls about all the millions of ways there are to be a girl, and all the things that girls can do.

THINK ABOUT

Do you see differences in how girls and boys are treated?

Do you think that it is fair?

MY *personal philosophy*

You are never too young to learn about feminism. If girls and boys understand the true meaning of the idea, and what it hopes to achieve, then we can work towards a world that is fair to everyone. And we all want that, right?

MY *favourite quote*

" *Women saying, "I'm not a feminist" is my greatest pet peeve. Do you believe that women should be paid the same for doing the same jobs? Do you believe that women should be allowed to leave the house? Do you think that women and men both deserve equal rights? Great, then you're a feminist.* **"**

Lena Dunham, actor and writer

MY *feminism*

LOUISE SPILSBURY

Louise Spilsbury studied women's writing at university and did a Masters degree in Women and Literature. She co-founded *Aurora*, a magazine featuring creative writing and illustrations by women, based in Liverpool. She then became an author, and has written more than 200 books for young people on a wide range of subjects.

BECOMING *a feminist*

Growing up, I loved watching old films with feisty female characters, and my favourite books were about adventurous girls – but in real life girls didn't seem to have the same chances or choices as boys. I felt annoyed when teachers suggested that, although I was as clever as the boys in my class, I should train to be their secretary – or when adults hinted that my job choices weren't important because I'd stop working if I got married. At university I learned about many wonderful female writers whose stories rarely get heard because of their gender. It was during that time when I discovered feminism.

WHAT *does feminism mean to me?*

Feminism is important to me because I believe treating women and men equally can make the world a better place for everyone. Some people would say that's a bit idealistic, but I believe that patriarchy holds us all back. For one thing, until women get the same chances to succeed in work and politics as men, the world is missing out on a lot of talent and insight.

I feel certain that when we have a more even balance of male and female leaders, the world will be a fairer and safer place. And feminism can help to stop the gender discrimination that affects men, too. For example, it's not fair that men have to hide their feelings for fear of being called 'weak', or be pressured to act tougher or more aggressive than they really feel.

Some people think that because there are laws about women's equality that there is no need for feminism any more. The facts say otherwise. For example, research commissioned by Girlguiding UK in 2015 found that two-thirds of girls believe women are still judged more on their looks than their ability, and one in three say that they are so worried about the way they look that they would consider plastic surgery. Facts like these make me both sad and angry at the same time, and remind me why feminism is still so important today.

MY *favourite quote*

There is a wonderful book called *We Should All Be Feminists* by the Nigerian writer Chimamanda Ngozi Adichie, which my daughter Hattie introduced me to. It sums up so much about what being a feminist means to me and I urge everyone to read it. This is one quote from it:

❝*We spend too much time teaching girls to worry about what boys think of them. But the reverse is not the case. We don't teach boys to care about being likable. We spend too much time telling girls that they cannot be angry or aggressive or tough, which is bad enough, but then we turn around and either praise or excuse men for the same reasons. All over the world, there are so many magazine articles and books telling women what to do, how to be and not to be, in order to attract or please men. There are far fewer guides for men about pleasing women.*❞

*P*eople had been talking about the issue of women's rights long before the word 'feminism' was used, or feminists started to campaign. For example, in 1792, a writer called Mary Wollstonecraft wrote a book, A Vindication of the Rights of Woman, in which she appealed for women and men to be given equal opportunities in education, work and politics. However, the word 'feminism' was first used in the 1890s, when more people began to get involved in the struggle for equal rights for women.

When did FEMINISM BEGIN?

FIRST-WAVE FEMINISM

Through history, the feminist movement has had periods of great activity, known as waves. The first wave of action began in the US in the1840s, when most women around the world had few rights. Early feminists campaigned for women to be educated, for better working conditions, for the right to own property and, if they got divorced, to be allowed to care for their children. However, their main focus was on women's right to vote. Women won the right to vote across America in 1920, and women over the age of 21 won the right to vote in the UK in 1928.

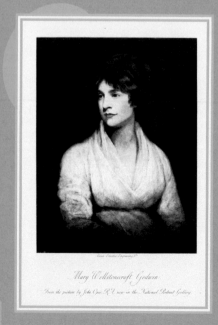

Mary Wollstonecraft Godwin

From the picture by John Opie R.A. now in the National Portrait Gallery

"I do not wish them (women) to have power over men; but over themselves."

Mary Wollstonecraft
Writer

SECOND-WAVE *feminism*

In the 1960s, a second wave of feminism began. The 'Women's Liberation Movement', as it was known, was explosive, and brought the idea of feminism to millions of women. The name came from an American author called Betty Friedan, who wrote an important book called *The Feminine Mystique*. In it she said that women had a right to be more than wives and mothers, if they wanted to – a radical idea at the time.

Through the 1960s and 1970s, into the 1980s, second-wave feminists fought for equal pay and better job opportunities for women. For example, their efforts brought in a law to stop employers sacking women when they became pregnant. They campaigned for more nurseries so that mothers could go out to work if they wanted to, and for more choices of contraception, so women could choose how many children they had and when they had them. They also began to campaign to end gender discrimination, or sexism, and for better laws to protect women from violence.

> **"** In almost every professional field, in business and in the arts and sciences, women are still treated as second-class citizens. It would be a great service to tell girls who plan to work in society to expect this subtle, uncomfortable discrimination – tell them not to be quiet, and hope it will go away, but fight it. A girl should not expect special privileges because of her sex, but neither should she 'adjust' to prejudice and discrimination. **"**

Betty Friedan,
Author of *The Feminine Mystique*

THIRD-WAVE FEMINISM

By the 1990s and into the 21st century, women's lives seemed to have changed for the better. In many countries women had more rights and career opportunities than ever before, and young women grew up expecting to have the freedom and choices that previous feminists had fought for and won. However, the problem of sexism still remained.

At the same time, people who were uncomfortable with women's new freedom created a negative image of feminism – parts of the media labelled feminists as ugly, aggressive and men-haters. Some women were also critical of second-wave feminists, who they said focused too much on the problems of women who were upper-middle class, married and white. This meant that many women started to reject the idea of feminism.

For people who fought against sexism in the third wave, their struggles were more individual. Third-wave feminists split into smaller groups campaigning for different things – changes for younger women, women from poor backgrounds and women of different nationalities, races and religions. Third-wave feminists also focused on changing stereotypes of women, for example by challenging the way women are presented in the media.

THINK ABOUT

What do you think when you hear the word 'feminism'?

Why do you think some people try to describe feminism as a bad thing?

How might this put people off calling themselves feminists?

❝*We cannot all succeed when half of us are held back.*❞

Malala Yousafzai
Female education activist

FOURTH-WAVE *feminism*

Lots of people think that we are living in the fourth wave of feminism right now. In the 21st century, many more people have begun to identify themselves as feminists, from Barack Obama to Beyoncé. European and American feminists are working with feminists in other parts of the world such as Asia, Africa and Latin America. The wide availability of the Internet and social media has also led to a huge increase in the number of feminist campaigns online.

Feminists today are working to encourage more women into politics, to get equal pay and to solve problems such as sexual harassment and violence against women. They are also trying to change the fact that women are often judged on the way they look rather than on who they are or what they do. Fourth-wave feminism has become mainstream, and it is no longer seen as extreme to talk about equal rights for women, as it was in the past.

"I don't know if we can talk about 'waves' of feminism any more – by my reckoning, the next wave would be the fifth, and I suspect it's around the fifth wave that you stop referring to individual waves, and start to refer, simply, to an incoming tide."

Caitlin Moran,
Writer

Does feminism MATTER TODAY?

Do we still need feminism in the 21st century? What do these statistics* tell us about women's lives across the planet today?

WORK

- Around the world, less than a quarter of the most powerful jobs in business are done by women.
- Only half of the women who could work do so, compared to three-quarters of men.
- Women earn less than men. For every pound earned by men, women earn between 70 and 90 pence.
- Less than four per cent of the world's 500 biggest companies are run by women.

POWER AND DECISION-MAKING

- Only 18 per cent of ministers appointed to governments across the world are female.
- There are more male than female judges in over half the countries of the world.
- Around the world only about a third of the people working in police forces are women.

EDUCATION

- Across the globe, more than 30 million girls of primary-school age are still not in school.
- Of all the people who cannot read in the world, more than two-thirds are girls and women.
- Fewer women than men study science and engineering at university, and only 30 per cent of researchers around the world are women.

* From The World Bank, and a United Nations report called 'The World's Women 2015', © United Nations 2015.

MEDIA

- Only seven per cent of films are directed by women.
- Female characters only make up about 20 per cent of the films we watch.
- Only 20 per cent of films are written by women.
- Almost 80 per cent of film producers are men.

FAMILY

- In 10 countries, women have to obey their husbands by law.
- In developing countries, about one in three married women has no control over household spending on major purchases.
- One in 10 married women does not get asked about how the money she earns is spent.

SEXISM in the UK*

- 81 per cent of girls and young women aged 11 to 21 reported that they had experienced some form of everyday sexism (such as hearing a sexist comment on TV) in a week.
- Three in five girls aged 13 to 21 have experienced sexual harassment at school, college or work.
- 85 per cent of girls aged 11 to 21 say they experience sexism in some aspect of their lives.

"Humanity requires both men and women, and we are equally important and need one another. So why are we viewed as less than equal? These old attitudes are drilled into us from the very beginning. We have to teach our boys the rules of equality and respect, so that as they grow up, gender equality becomes a natural way of life. And we have to teach our girls that they can reach as high as humanly possible."

Beyoncé Knowles-Carter,
Singer and actor

* These facts come from the Girlguiding Girls' Attitudes Survey 2015.

Why is it important for women to have the right to vote in elections, and for there to be female ministers and leaders in governments? It's important because it allows women to be involved in making the laws and decisions that affect their lives.

FEMINISM *and* POLITICS

VOTES FOR WOMEN!

In Britain the campaigns for women's suffrage, or the right to vote, began in the late 19th century. The suffragists, under the leadership of Millicent Fawcett (above, left), believed in peaceful tactics such as marches to prove that women could be responsible enough to vote. The suffragettes, led by Emmeline Pankhurst (above, right), carried out more extreme protests to make their voices heard, such as breaking windows and chaining themselves to fences. During the First World War (1914–1918), women had to take over men's jobs while the men were away fighting. It meant that women were seen as more capable than they had been before, and interest in women's rights grew. In 1918, women over 30 won the right to vote in the UK, and by 1928, women over 21 could vote too. However, it took some countries much longer to give women the right to vote. Women in Switzerland couldn't vote until 1971, and Saudi Arabia only gave women the vote in 2015.

WOMEN IN *politics*

Today, more women around the world participate in government and politics than ever before, and some countries have even had female leaders. Yet, there are still fewer women than men voting in elections or becoming politicians. This means that the different perspectives and experiences of up to 50 per cent of the world's population are not being heard.

For a country to be successful, it needs the best people in its government. If politicians are only being chosen from half the population, that means some governments are missing out on a lot of female talent.

Female politicians who work on women's issues bring about changes that help everyone, too. For example, equal pay for women means whole families are better off.

Feminists campaign to get more women into politics and make it easier for women to work in governments. Politicians tend to work very long hours, which is hard for mothers to do. So, feminists are campaigning for changes to working hours to help them. In some countries there are laws guaranteeing a certain percentage of women in government, to make sure that they are fairly represented.

> **"***If a country doesn't recognize minority rights and human rights, including women's rights, you will not have the kind of stability and prosperity that is possible.***"**
>
> Hillary Clinton,
> American politician

THINK ABOUT

What do you think might be the result of there being unequal numbers of men and women in government?

Do you think there should be equal numbers of men and women in governments?

MY *feminism* DAWN O'PORTER

Author, TV presenter and journalist Dawn O'Porter brings her belief in women's equality into all of her work – even her job as a fashion designer.

IN THE PAST, YOU HAVE SAID THAT FEMINISM IS MORE THAN A WORD, IT'S AN ACTION. *What do you mean by that?*

Feminism means to me what it should mean to everyone – equalisation of the sexes. Men are not better or more powerful than women, and they shouldn't be paid more for doing the same job. Feminism is about getting that straight, but a lot of people don't seem to have got that message yet. And yes, I think to call yourself a feminist you should be active. You should talk about it, spread the word, and be it. I don't think it's enough to just say you are a feminist, you have to actively live it.

WHEN YOU'RE WRITING FICTION, DO YOU THINK ABOUT EQUALITY WHEN YOU *create the characters?*

Massively, but I want to be honest. I don't want to feel I have to write women characters that don't care about beauty and love and babies just so I don't write 'typical' female characters. I'm tough, but my marriage and child are everything to me. I'd drop everything for them, of course. But I also want to be honest about women – we don't just care about love and babies, there is a lot more to life. My job as a writer is to represent how women feel, and being honest about the things we want is all a part of that. I want to be inclusive and make sure that I represent the world I live in. It's so important for writers to do that.

YOU HAVE A LITTLE BOY. WHAT WILL YOU TEACH HIM *about feminism?*

Very little. What I will teach him is that power doesn't make the man. That he must, and can, talk about his feelings. That he is not above women and that he must respect them. I'm not going to raise him to be a feminist, I'm going to raise him to be a really, really great guy. I'll do the same if I have a girl next time. And that will be how we stamp out gender inequality in the future.

YOU HAVE JUST LAUNCHED YOUR OWN FASHION RANGE. HOW HAVE YOUR *feminist beliefs affected the clothes?*

It's all about making women feel good. Empowering them. I don't design clothes that I believe make women attractive, I design clothes that women love, and therefore make them feel powerful. I believe that clothes help you be the person you need to be that day, so the way fashion makes you think is a lot more interesting to me than just how it looks. How does this dress make this woman feel? That's the question I ask. Will this help her move forward? Fashion can do that. It's very powerful.

In 1900, many women in the UK stayed at home while their husbands went out to work. Some unmarried middle-class women worked as teachers, and working-class women often worked long hours for low pay as maids and servants. After the First World War, however, when women proved they could do jobs such as ship-building and driving ambulances, things began to change...

Feminism
AND WORK

In the 1920s, laws were passed allowing women to work in careers they hadn't been able to before. At last, they could become lawyers, accountants and politicians. However, women were not paid the same as men for doing the same jobs. It wasn't until 1968, when female workers at the Ford car factory in Dagenham went on strike over equal pay, that the Equal Pay Act was passed in the UK. This law meant that women and men doing the same job had to be given the same pay.

THINK ABOUT

Do you think women and men should get paid the same for doing the same job?

Do you think women could or should be able to do all the jobs men do?

Even after the laws were changed, many women could not get the jobs they applied for because some people still thought that they couldn't do jobs that were usually done by men. Women had to take companies to court to get the jobs they wanted. For example, in the 1970s an American woman called Brenda Berkman sued the New York fire service for gender discrimination when it refused to let her become a firefighter. After she won the case she, and 40 other women, joined the force and Brenda later went on to become a fire captain.

WORKING WOMEN *today*

Today women can do most of the jobs men do, but not all. For example, in some countries female soldiers aren't allowed to fight on the front line, and in China women are discouraged from becoming miners or naval engineers. Across the world many women still face discrimination, and unequal pay and opportunities. What else prevents women from being equal to men at work?

One problem is that even though girls do well at school, they are not always confident as leaders. This is partly because girls tend to be encouraged to be gentle and modest and discouraged from taking the lead. In 2014, Sheryl Sandberg, the Chief Operating Officer of Facebook, started a campaign called 'Ban Bossy' to stop people calling girls 'bossy' when they act confidently, and to encourage them to take the lead.

Another problem is that until there are more women in senior jobs it is hard for girls to imagine themselves doing those jobs. If you have never seen a female pilot, how can you want to be one? Feminists encourage women to tell their stories of success to girls, so that girls can learn about jobs they could do.

❝ *Women have made tons of progress. But we still have a small percentage of the top jobs in any industry, in any nation in the world. I think that's partly because from a very young age, we encourage our boys to lead and we call our girls bossy.* **❞**

Sheryl Sandberg,
Chief Operating Officer of Facebook

MY *feminism*
JULIE BENTLEY

As head of Girlguiding in the UK, Julie Bentley is in charge of more than half a million girls across the nation.

WHAT DOES FEMINISM *mean to you?*

For me it's simply about boys and girls and men and women having equality in their lives – at work and in their private lives. Having the same opportunities and being paid the same for doing the same job. The word has been incorrectly associated with meaning women think they're better than men, or don't like men. That's very unfortunate as true feminism is about men and women having an equal place in the world.

HAVE YOU EVER EXPERIENCED *sexism at work?*

When I was younger I experienced what I would call 'lazy sexism'. So if a man came to the office he might think I was the secretary rather than the boss. Or sometimes I was referred to as scary or aggressive and when I asked them why, it was just because I was being direct or challenging. My response would be: "Do you think you would have used that word about a man behaving the same way?" I would ask them to think about their assumptions and question them.

WHY ARE WOMEN STILL
underrepresented in top jobs?

Young women that I meet often say that if they don't see enough women in those jobs, they then think it's not possible for a girl to aim for that.

We need to have strong messages in society saying that women can do those jobs, starting at school. When girls are talked to about what careers they want, we need to speak to them in the same way we do with boys. At the moment, far fewer girls will say that they want to be engineers, but that's not because they wouldn't be capable – it's because they don't see that as a girl's job.

As women get older, there is also the challenge of parenting. Until it becomes the norm for as many men as women to take six months off work to look after a new baby, then it's going to be a challenge. We need laws that recognise men and women as equal in parenting responsibilities. Until then, we will always have a challenge getting women into high-level positions, because they

are still seen as the primary carer and our current structure is based around that.

Women make up 50 per cent of the population but they're not equally represented in the top jobs. That happens in all areas of work. In the charity sector the majority of the workforce are women, but look at the the bosses and the majority are men.

WHAT DO YOU SAY TO YOUNG WOMEN ABOUT *their future careers?*

There are no barriers – you can be what you want to be. Have confidence to believe in you. You can do a job that's not a traditional woman's career. Think bigger and wider. It is also fine to have a more traditional role, but the most important thing is that you have the choice.

"I'm a feminist. I've been a female for a long time now. It'd be stupid not to be on my own side."

Maya Angelou,
Writer

Feminism and
THE MEDIA

*F*eminists believe that the way women are portrayed on TV, in adverts, films and other forms of media affects our ideas about how women should behave, how they should look and what they should do with their lives.

WOMEN IN ADVERTISING

For a long time, women in adverts were mostly shown as housewives – cooking, cleaning and getting excited about new cleaning products or gadgets. This began in the 1950s, when governments around the world encouraged women to leave work in order to free up jobs for men who'd returned from the Second World War (1939–1945). Adverts still use female stereotypes to sell things today. Some seem to suggest that all a woman should care about is being pretty or shopping for clothes, while men are more often shown as successful businessmen and sportsmen, or driving fast, expensive cars. This is changing, however, and today more adverts show men and women in less stereotyped roles.

THINK ABOUT

Do you think the way the media presents men and women is always fair and true?

Have you noticed a difference in the way adverts show boys and girls or men and women?

WOMEN *on screen*

Most films and TV shows have boys or men in the leading roles, and action heroes and the main villains in films are usually male. On screen, girls and women often only play supporting roles to the male leads, or characters whose main interest in life is finding a boyfriend or husband.

Thanks to feminism, things are changing. There are more films being made with strong and interesting female leads. Recently children's film-maker Disney was praised for the film *Frozen*, which stars two sisters who don't need a prince to rescue them.

However, the lack of female writers, film directors and producers means that most film-makers are still male and most films give men the leading roles and show women as stereotypes. This is a problem because if, for example, films always show quiet, pretty girls as heroines and angry or bossy girls getting into trouble, it's just another way of telling women how they should behave.

> **❝***Where are the female stories? Where are they? Where are the directors, where are the writers? It's imbalanced, so given that we are half the cinema-going public, we are half the people [who] watch drama or watch anything else, where is that?* **❞**

Keira Knightley,
Actor

> **❝***The education and empowerment of women throughout the world cannot fail to result in a more caring, tolerant, just and peaceful life for all.* **❞**

Aung San Suu Kyi,
Politician and activist

ARE THINGS CHANGING?

Yes, in some ways. On TV there are more women working as presenters and newsreaders and more female experts being asked for their opinions. Female sports commentators are more common today and, even though most airtime is given to men's sports, more women's sports are being shown on TV. For example, in the UK in 2015, women's World Cup football was shown by the BBC.

However, there are still problems. Although there are more female presenters, most are slim, young and pretty, while looks and age aren't as much of a consideration for male presenters. And while male sportsmen are asked about their training, skills or success in interviews, female athletes are often asked about their looks, clothes or relationships.

THINK ABOUT

What do you think happens when all women on screen look a certain way?

Do you think male and female athletes should be asked the same questions in interviews?

❝ *My hope for the future, in every young girl I meet, is that they all realize their worth and ask for it.* **❞**

Taylor Swift,
Singer-songwriter

SOCIAL MEDIA

Today, many campaigners use the media to promote feminism. For example, social-media websites have become a really important tool for helping feminists to make changes and launch campaigns. Huge numbers of women have shown their support for feminism and joined the conversation about women's rights on Twitter, Instagram and Facebook, a trend known as 'hashtag feminism'. In 2012, Laura Bates founded a website called the Everyday Sexism Project. Since her campaign started, millions of women have contacted her to record their experiences of sexism, from disrespectful comments to illegal abuse.

At the Oscars awards ceremony in 2015, many famous actors supported a hashtag on social media called #askhermore. The hashtag encouraged journalists to ask women the same interesting questions that the men were asked, rather than about their clothes. Actor Reese Witherspoon was a supporter of the campaign and posted on Instagram a list of questions that reporters could ask instead.

❝Because so many more women are standing up and talking about these issues it enables other people to stand up too ... And the more who add their voices, the harder it is to shout us down.❞

Laura Bates,
Writer and founder of the Everyday Sexism Project

MY *feminism*
GEMMA CAIRNEY

BBC Radio 1's Gemma Cairney talks to us about why she cares so much about equality for boys and girls.

WHAT DOES FEMINISM *mean to you?*

Taking it back to basics, being a feminist means that I am proud of who I am. I am a female, and that makes me proud.

WHY DO SOME PEOPLE NOT LIKE TO CALL *themselves feminists?*

I think the word is the problem. People get confused by language sometimes. The word 'feminist' has been around for a long time and means different things to different people. I think that makes it a really wonderful word because it means so much, and it's fine to have different opinions. People don't always like to brand themselves with such big words, but they might be a feminist without realising. Feminism just means total equality and a love and respect for women.

WHAT DO YOU THINK ABOUT SO MANY FAMOUS WOMEN COMING OUT TO *support feminism now?*

It's great that so many popular young women have openly called themselves feminists. And even though it means different things to different people, I think it's a good thing to discuss and take control of. Beyoncé singing feminist lyrics is very powerful. I'm really happy to talk about fourth-wave feminism, even if people come to loggerheads.

HOW DO YOU THINK THAT SOCIAL MEDIA HAS *affected feminism?*

It's been a really good meeting place for lots of conversations about a demand for equality.

If there's a big issue that makes people feel a lot and makes them want to speak out, social media gives them the opportunity to do that. Speaking out is excellent. And it's good to ask questions. It's good to be honest. It's good to stand up for your rights and to seek guidance through social media, but sometimes it can get a bit noisy!

HOW DO YOU FEEL ABOUT HOW THE MEDIA *represents women?*

When I think of the biggest billboards and covers of magazines, or the most watched YouTube videos, I know that not everyone we see is in control of the images that are put out. There is a huge team behind them helping them look like that. Women are made to focus on their looks too much, and are often talked about because of the way they look or dress above anything else that they do. There needs to be different representations of people in the media. We can make that happen – we can take control of the Internet. It's up to us to put out positive imagery. We can create greatness online! Be free to be yourself. That for me epitomises feminism – to feel like you can be you is a great start. Our identities as girls are stamped on us from a young age, but we are so many things. Know who you are and everything you've got to offer. You can look however you want to look, and be however you want to be – that is a really strong and mighty thing to have inside of you.

In countries such as the UK, girls have the same right to an education as boys. However, there are still problems caused by gender discrimination. In the past people were brought up to believe that men were better at science and maths than women. There is no evidence to back this up, but it has been said so often that today, many girls still lack confidence in maths and science. This results in fewer women studying subjects such as engineering and construction, which means they are missing out on chances to work in different jobs and the country is missing out on talent.

Feminism and EDUCATION

In some regions of the world, girls still do not have the same access to education as boys. In Sub-Saharan Africa, it's estimated that it will be 2086 before all girls complete primary-school education. In some countries girls are taken out of school early to get married or to work at home, and there are people who believe girls should not have an education. This is wrong because when girls are educated, they lead healthier and more productive lives. They gain the skills and self-confidence they need to get jobs that help them and their families escape poverty.

THINK ABOUT

Do you think that girls and boys are treated the same at school?

Do you think boys are better than girls at certain subjects?

**"Here's to strong women.
May we know them.
May we be them.
May we raise them."**

Unknown

MALALA'S *Story*

Malala Yousafzai was born in 1997 in Mingora, Pakistan. During her early life, the Taliban, an extreme Islamist group, tried to take control of the area where she lived. They believed that girls should not go to school – they even blew up girls' schools.

Malala went to a school that her father, Ziauddin Yousafzai, had started. Malala's father believes educating girls is important and encouraged her to speak out. In September 2008, Malala gave a talk in Peshawar, Pakistan, called 'How dare the Taliban take away my basic right to education?' She also started blogging for the BBC about her struggle for an education.

This angered the Taliban and in 2012, Taliban members boarded Malala's school bus and shot her. Malala nearly died and had to be flown to the UK for life-saving medical treatment. However, the attack didn't stop Malala, and in 2013 she gave a speech at the UN about girls' education. In October 2014, at the age of 17, Malala became the youngest person ever to receive the Nobel Peace Prize for her campaigning for the right of all children to education.

"I saw a young girl selling oranges. She was scratching marks on a piece of paper with a pencil to account for the oranges she had sold, as she could not read or write. I took a photo of her and vowed I would do everything in my power to help educate girls just like her. This was the war I was going to fight."

Malala Yousafzai,
Female education activist

MY *feminism* ADORA SVITAK

Adora Svitak is an 18-year-old American author and activist. She was a child prodigy and at seven years old was called the World's Cleverest Child. She wrote and published her first book at just 13, and has spoken around the world on education and feminism.

WHAT DOES FEMINISM *mean to you?*

To me, feminism is the dictionary definition: the advocacy of women's rights on the grounds of political, social, and economic equality to men. I also think it's important for feminism to be intersectional, considering the extent to which oppression is magnified by other factors like race or socio-economic status, since gender and its privileges or disadvantages don't exist in a vacuum.

WHY DO WE STILL *need feminism?*

We still need feminism because little girls still don't get to experience the world as fully and fearlessly as little boys. We get told to cover up more, stay quieter, be nicer.

Sexism is visible everywhere, from college campuses to workplaces where women lose financially for becoming mothers, to television shows and movies where women (especially women of colour) have complex character development, speaking roles, and their own storylines much less frequently than men.

WHY DO WE NEED A BOOK LIKE THIS TEACHING FEMINISM TO *young people?*

A lot of young people don't encounter feminism until they're teenagers browsing Tumblr or maybe hearing about celebrities like Beyoncé or Taylor Swift declaring themselves feminists in magazine interviews. It's important to engage with feminism from a much earlier age, since the attitudes that we develop as children are crucial to how we behave in later life.

Feminism teaches important skills, like questioning gender roles, respecting others, and observing where society is unfair. Learning about feminism makes you a better human being.

WHEN DID YOU FIRST BECOME INTERESTED IN *women's equality?*

I first became interested in women's equality as a young child, because my parents bought me books about women leaders (queens, first ladies, scientists, etc.) that I devoured. I remember reading one, about Elizabeth Blackwell (the first woman to receive a medical degree in the United States), and realizing that women in her time faced significantly more obstacles to gaining an education or entering certain fields than I did. That made me interested in what had changed and what still needed changing.

THROUGHOUT THE WORLD THERE IS STILL A GENDER EQUALITY GAP IN EDUCATION. WHAT IS YOUR VIEW ON THIS? *What can be done to solve the problem?*

In some countries, deciding not to educate girls is simply an economic decision: boys are seen as potential wage-earners, while girls are seen as future wives and mothers. Shifting families' visions of what girls can grow up to become is a vital first step to promoting equal education of girls and boys. This can be done through increasing diverse media representations of women. For instance, Sheryl Sandberg's LeanIn.org and Getty Images partnered to create the 'Lean In' stock-photo collection, seeking to rectify the problem of a lack of diversity in images of women by providing pictures of women (of all ages and ethnicities) weightlifting, skateboarding, leading board meetings, and more. Such moves are first steps to challenging long-held notions about what women can do.

Throughout history, society has had different ideas of what a woman's perfect shape should be. The ideal women of the 1600s and 1700s were plump and rounded. In the 1800s, women wore corsets to make their waists tiny. By the 1920s, the ideal shape was thin and flat-chested, so some women bound their chests. In the 1950s, women were supposed to be curvy again. The image of what an ideal woman was and is expected to look like is usually represented by the models used in adverts and magazines, and it keeps changing!

Feminism and
BODY IMAGE

When we look at the changing ideas about what women should look like, it seems obvious that these images can only ever present a very narrow idea of what is beautiful. In reality people come in a variety of heights, weights, sizes and skin colours, and always should do and will. Feminists began tackling the issue of women's body image in the 1800s when they campaigned against the tight corsets that caused breathing and digestive problems. They have continued to argue against limiting ideas of beauty ever since.

THINK ABOUT

When you look at a magazine, do all the models in adverts look very similar?

Do you think that the images of models in magazines represent what women really look like?

MAKING *progress*

Most feminists believe that although fashion can be fun and it's good to take care of yourself, there is still too much emphasis placed on the way women look. They are trying to change things for the better. For example, some feminists have been putting pressure on advertisers and magazines to use female models that are an average size, and to stop airbrushing pictures.

In 2012, Julia Bluhm, a 14-year-old schoolgirl from Maine, USA, petitioned *Seventeen* magazine to stop Photoshopping models' images, as she believed that this had a big effect on girls and how they feel about themselves.

If women are looking at fake images of perfect models, they need to know that the people in the pictures aren't real and they shouldn't expect to look like them! Julia got more than 86,000 people to sign her petition and succeeded in persuading the magazine to change how it produces photographs.

In 2015, France passed a law banning models that are very underweight from being allowed to feature in magazines or fashion shows. They have also passed a law saying that there must be a warning on any images where the the model has been digitally altered or improved.

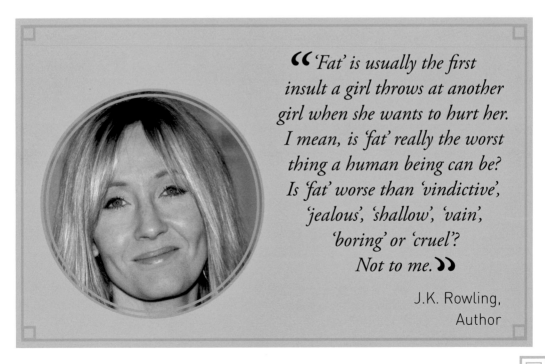

" *'Fat' is usually the first insult a girl throws at another girl when she wants to hurt her. I mean, is 'fat' really the worst thing a human being can be? Is 'fat' worse than 'vindictive', 'jealous', 'shallow', 'vain', 'boring' or 'cruel'? Not to me.* **"**

J.K. Rowling,
Author

MY *feminism* LAUREN LAVERNE

She's a DJ, TV presenter, author, singer and comedian.
Oh, and Lauren Laverne is also a feminist!

WHAT DOES FEMINISM *mean to you?*

It is about gender equality. It's a way of looking at the world and how we can make women socially, culturally, economically and politically equal to men, which would benefit men and women alike.

HOW LONG HAVE YOU BEEN *interested in feminism?*

I was brought up by a feminist! We had a very equal household. In many ways I think that was the most useful and important instruction of all. Then as I got older and as everyone's does, my life became more complicated. I actually started to get a few knocks and experience sexism and misogyny myself – that led me to look into it more deeply and find out more about it. It's inspiring but frustrating to see women 100 years ago naming the problems, fighting the same battles and to look at how far we have to go ... but also important to realise how far we have come.

WHY DO YOU THINK IT'S IMPORTANT FOR YOUNG PEOPLE TO LEARN ABOUT FEMINISM?

Because they deserve a better world, and they might have to help build it. Inequality harms everyone - not just women. Men and boys are also disadvantaged by a system which piles expectations and restrictions on them, and doesn't allow women to be equal participants and partners in running the world. I am a mother of two sons and I want equality on their behalf too.

A fairer world would also be a richer one – Oxfam has done research which showed how much richer most countries would be if societies were more equal. In some countries that means reducing maternal mortality rates, in ours it might mean closing the pay gap (which isn't set to close for another 70 years) – there are so many ways all of us could improve, and everyone could benefit.

WHY IS THE SUBJECT OF WOMEN'S BODIES SO IMPORTANT FOR FEMINISTS?

Women's bodies are the battleground for so much of this stuff – literally and metaphorically. Our bodies are still subject to extreme forms of patriarchal control, but less obvious forms of control like body-shaming and telling women how they should look or what they should wear are part of the same problem. Women must have control over their own bodies – it's the first step to equality and in so many ways we still haven't taken it.

WHAT CHANGES WOULD YOU LIKE TO SEE IN HOW WOMEN'S BODIES ARE TREATED?

I believe in what some writers call the body-positive movement. I enjoy fashion and beauty as tools for self-expression, affirmation, creativity and fun, but I don't think they should be compulsory, and I hate the fact that women are judged on how they look. I'm not always interested in how I look – and even on the days I am, it's not the most important thing. When it comes to fashion and stuff the only currency I believe in is ideas, really. I'm much more interested in what you're *saying* with what you're wearing than in whether your thighs meet in the middle or not.

Sorting out the STEREOTYPES

*S*tereotypes begin as soon as babies are born, when people buy blue clothes for boys and pink clothes for girls. This gender discrimination usually continues with the type of toys and books children are given. While little girls are often given dolls, princess costumes and play kitchens, little boys tend to get toys such as cars, chemistry sets and toolkits.

THINK ABOUT

Do you think girls and boys should be given the same toys when they are babies?

Do you think if girls and boys were treated the same when they were little they would be different when they were older?

At home, some girls find that they are asked to help tidy the house more often than boys, while boys may help more with chores such as fixing things. These stereotypes tend to encourage boys to be more interested in engineering, building and adventure and girls to focus more on clothes, their appearance and looking after the home. When stereotypes start this young, is it any wonder that they continue as people grow up?

Stereotypes are damaging because they can stop people from doing the things they want to do or are good at. That's why feminists want to make people aware of how these stereotypes work and to try to avoid them.

BOYS CAN BE *feminists too*

Gender stereotypes don't just affect girls. Feminism is about equality and fairness, which affects men and women. Everyone should be free to make their own choices. Just like women, men have a variety of talents and should be allowed to use them to do all kinds of jobs. Today more men are able to do jobs that were once thought to be for women only, such as being nurses, nannies, secretaries and nail technicians.

Because of changing attitudes, men can now take time off work during the first weeks after their baby is born, too.

If women are paid an equal wage, the father in a family might be able to work less and see their children more.

Gender stereotypes affect our mental health as well. In the past, girls were encouraged to talk about their feelings while boys and men were told it wasn't a masculine thing to do. A lot of people even thought that it was not okay for boys to cry! Today more people understand that it is as important for boys and men to experience and express emotions as it is for girls and women.

❝ *We know that when women are empowered, they immeasurably improve the lives of everyone around them – their families, their communities, and their countries ... This is not just about women, we men need to recognise the part we play too.* **❞**

Prince Harry

MY *feminism*
BEN BAILEY SMITH (AKA DOC BROWN)

So can men really be feminists? They can! And comedian, actor and rapper Doc Brown tells us why.

ARE YOU A *feminist?*

Yes, 100 per cent! To me it means belief in equal rights for men and women and I don't understand how you couldn't be a feminist. People are just scared of the word. They don't really understand it and they feel like there are bad connotations attached to it, but I just take it as a given that everyone believes in equality. When people hear the word 'feminist' they think: 'I'm not one of these women who burn their underwear and beat men around the head with truncheons.' That's what they think it is! But it's just a lack of education, really. In my stand-up I say to the audience: 'You are all feminists!'

People feel threatened by things that they don't understand. Women who are scared of the word 'feminist' are very strange to me. It feels like they're afraid of being associated with radicals, but it's not radical to want equality for the human race. They worry that they'll be left out at work, or that men will think that they're not feminine. That's just nonsense. And I think feminism makes some men afraid of losing power.

YOU HAVE TWO DAUGHTERS. DOES THAT CHANGE HOW YOU FEEL ABOUT *equality for women?*

I was always a well-rounded individual who had respect for the opposite sex, but having daughters makes you think about it more. I tell my daughters every day: 'Don't ever consider yourself less than a man'. I've seen the battles start so early. For example, my seven-year-old loves comics and superheroes, but when she wears her Batman trainers to school, or her DC-comics hat, she's been told that they're for boys. That makes me furious. But some boys once challenged her on her Spider-Man knowledge and she won. The boys were completely dumbfounded, and I was very proud of her.

HAVE MEN BENEFITED FROM *feminism?*

We will all benefit from living in a world where everyone feels that they can achieve the same regardless of their sex, background, ethnicity or social standing. If you live in a community where all those people feel they can achieve you will benefit from living in a happy community.

> **❝ All men should be feminists. If men care about women's rights, the world will be a better place. ❞**
>
> John Legend,
> Singer-songwriter

DO YOU TRY TO HAVE AN EQUAL *family?*

I took time off to raise my first child while my wife was working as a teacher. I didn't find it easy but I didn't feel emasculated either – it was a unique and fun element of my life to be a stay-at-home dad. It can never be taken away from me that I was there at that crucial time. Why wouldn't you want to do that if you can?

What DO YOU THINK?

Now that you've read the book, what do you think feminists and non-feminists agree on? What are the most important issues feminists deal with?

Here are some questions we've raised:

Introducing feminism

Where have you heard the word 'feminism' before? How was it used? What would you like to know about it?

WHAT IS A FEMINIST?

What do you think when you hear the word feminism?

Why do you think some people try to describe feminism as a bad thing?

How might this put people off calling themselves feminists?

Does feminism matter today?

What do you think about women's equality today? Do you think there is still work for feminists to do?

FEMINISM AND POLITICS

What do you think might be the result of there being unequal numbers of men and women in government?

Do you think there should be equal numbers of men and women in governments?

FEMINISM AND WORK

Do you think women and men should get paid the same for doing the same job?

Do you think women could or should be able to do all the jobs men do?

FEMINISM AND THE MEDIA

Do you think the way the media presents men and women is always fair and true?

Have you noticed a difference in the way adverts show boys and girls or men and women?

What do you think happens when women are objectified?

Do you think male and female athletes should be asked the same questions in interviews?

FEMINISM AND EDUCATION

Do you think that girls and boys are treated the same at school?

Do you think boys are better than girls at certain subjects?

FEMINISM AND BODY IMAGE

When you look at a magazine, do all the models in adverts look very similar?

Do you think that the images of models in magazines represent what women really look like?

Some people say advertisers should use normal people and stop altering models' photos. What do you think?

SORTING OUT THE STEREOTYPES

Do you think girls and boys should be given the same toys when they are babies?

Do you think if girls and boys were treated the same when they were little they would be different when they were older?

THINKING ABOUT FEMINISM

You've thought about a lot of questions throughout the book, but here are a few final big ones to consider …
How do you think that a girl's life today is different from her mother's life or her grandmother's life? Why do you think things are different for girls today? If you could change how women and girls are treated today, what would you do?

WHAT CAN WE DO?

Feminists have brought about great changes in the last 100 years, and in most countries there have been huge improvements in equal opportunities and rights for girls and women. However, there are still many problems caused by gender discrimination and in some countries women are still fighting for basic equal rights with men.

For those of us who do live in countries where equal rights are law, we must cherish that freedom and do all that we can to protect it. Feminists who fought for the vote, for women to have equal pay, or to be allowed into any careers, were fighting to help us all. They were fighting for men and women, and for a world where everyone is treated equally and fairness prevails. And that's what we all want, isn't it?

USEFUL *information*

If you would like to know more about feminism and women's rights today, take a look at these websites.

UN Women
http://www.unwomen.org/

Amy Poehler's Smart Girls
http://amysmartgirls.com/

A Mighty Girl
http://www.amightygirl.com/

The Female Lead
http://www.thefemalelead.com/

FURTHER *reading*

Here are some more great fiction and non-fiction books about feminism and amazing women ...

Girls are Best by Sandi Toksvig (Red Fox, 2009)

The Breadwinner by Deborah Ellis (OUP, 2014)

Girls Think of Everything by Catherine Thimmesh (Houghton Mifflin, 2002)

Girls Who Rocked the World by Michelle Roehm McCann and Amelie Welden (Beyond Words Publishing, 2012)

My Story: Suffragette by Carol Drinkwater (Scholastic, 2011)

The Girl Who Circumnavigated Fairyland in a Ship of Her Own Making by Catherynne M. Valente (Much-in-Little, 2013)

glossary

advocacy supporting, recommending or speaking up in favour of something.

affirmation a declaration or statement that something is right.

airbrushing digitally altering a photograph to make it look better.

campaign to work in an organised and active way to produce a particular result.

contraception a method to prevent pregnancy.

developing country a poor country working towards becoming more advanced.

diversity being different, or varied.

emasculated made to feel unmanly.

empowerment being empowered – having control over your life and actions.

equality being equal to others in rights, choices and opportunities.

feminine having qualities traditionally associated with being a girl or woman.

feminism the belief that men and women should have equal rights and opportunities.

human rights freedom of some kind that all people are entitled to. For example, human rights include the right to life, equality, and a fair trial, freedom from slavery and torture, and freedom of thought and expression.

intersectional overlapping two areas of interest.

Islamist a supporter of a political movement that wants to reorder government and society in accordance with laws defined by the religion of Islam.

masculine having qualities traditionally associated with a man.

objectification treating a person (usually a woman) as an object and not a person with their own thoughts, ideas and feelings.

prejudice an unfair feeling of dislike for a person or group because of race, sex or religion.

sexual harassment frequent, hostile attacks on a person because of their gender, such as inappropriate touching or nasty remarks about women in general.

socio-economic being caused by, or related to, both social and economic factors.

stereotype a generalisation made about people, for example that men are better drivers then women.

suffrage the right to vote in political elections.

vindictive the desire for revenge.

Index